Rabbit and Coyote

by Gustavo Juana

Illustrated by
Dawn Marie Pavloski

PEARSON

Scott
Foresman

Editorial Offices: Glenview, Illinois • Parsippany, New Jersey • New York, New York
Sales Offices: Needham, Massachusetts • Duluth, Georgia • Glenview, Illinois
Coppell, Texas • Sacramento, California • Mesa, Arizona

Coyote liked to chase Rabbit all
day long. Rabbit liked to play tricks on
Coyote all day long. They never got tired
of playing their games together.

One day, Coyote couldn't find Rabbit.
Then he saw Rabbit walking in a canyon.
This was a perfect place for chasing
Rabbit. The canyon walls were very high.
Rabbit couldn't escape.

Coyote followed Rabbit into the canyon. Rabbit saw Coyote behind her. *I am in trouble now,* Rabbit thought. *What can I do?* She ran. Coyote chased her. Rabbit hid in the canyon.

Finally, Coyote found Rabbit. Rabbit
was leaning against the canyon wall.
   "Quick, help me," Rabbit cried. "The
wall will fall on both of us!" A few small
rocks fell. Coyote ran to Rabbit and
helped her to hold up the canyon wall.

canyon wall

They held up the wall all night long. They got hungry. Rabbit saw a reflection of the moon in the pond. It looked like cheese. "I will drink all the water from the pond," Rabbit said. "Then we can eat that cheese in the water."

Rabbit drank some of the water. "This will never work," she said. "I will get some real food for us." She ran off. Coyote didn't follow. He was afraid the wall would fall on him.

Coyote got so hungry that he ran
away from the canyon wall. The wall
didn't fall. "Rabbit tricked me! I will
have some cheese, and then I will chase
her," Coyote said.

He drank all the water from the
pond. But he never found any cheese.
He was too full of water to move. He
couldn't chase Rabbit that day!